John André

**The Cow Chace**

A Poem in three Cantos

John André

**The Cow Chace**
*A Poem in three Cantos*

ISBN/EAN: 9783337180843

Printed in Europe, USA, Canada, Australia, Japan

Cover: Foto ©Thomas Meinert / pixelio.de

More available books at **www.hansebooks.com**

THE

# Cow Chace,

A

## POEM IN THREE CANTOS.

BY

Major JOHN ANDRE,

ADJUTANT GENERAL TO THE BRITISH ARMY
IN NEW YORK, IN 1780.

ALBANY, N. Y.:
J. MUNSELL, 78 STATE STREET.
1866.

*No.*—

EDITION 100 COPIES.

# PREFACE.

HE ſatirical Poem of Major Andre, entitled *The Cow Chace*, has been regarded with additional Intereſt from its being among the Laſt of the Writings of this talented but indiſcreet young Officer. It is founded upon an unſucceſsful Attempt of a Party under General Wayne, to Capture a Block-houſe upon the Hudſon in New Jerſey, and but a ſhort Diſtance from the City of New York, on the 21ſt of July, 1780.

This Blockhouſe was held by a ſmall Party of Loyaliſt Refugees, under Colonel Cuyler, but at this Time under the immediate Command of Captain Thomas Ward, and was built to cover the Operations of ſome Wood cutters employed in the Vicinity.

## Preface.

The prefent Edition is printed from the firft, as it appeared at Intervals in the Columns of Rivington's Royal Gazette, of New York City. The original Notes as printed in that Paper, are here preferved as Foot Notes, while all the additional Notes are given at the End, with the Authorities from whence derived.

This Poem has been often printed, and from the firft, has enjoyed a certain Degree of Popularity. Mr. Sargent in his Life of Andre intimates, that the Theme may have been fuggefted by the Fact, that the Author then boarded with John Thompfon, the Wood-cutting Agent at New York, and then engaged at this Place. The Piece is faid to have been written at Head-Quarters No. 1 Broadway. Dunlap reports, that the Printer received the laft Canto from the Author, on the Day before he fet out to meet Arnold.

The Army under General Wafhington lay at this Time in New Jerfey, a few Miles back from the River, in Bergen County, in

Pofition to obferve the Enemy, but too weak for any aggreffive Movement. The Americans were in great Want of the common Neceffaries of Life, many of the Soldiers were barefooted, moft of them ragged, and not a few bitterly complaining under their Privations, and apparently on the Verge of Mutiny.

The Expectation of an early Arrival of Troops from France, imparted Hope to the Continental Army, and the Difcontent which they fometimes expreffed, was in no Degree ftimulated by a Defire to return to the Britifh Allegiance.

To relieve their Wants by drawing from the Supplies within the Enemy's reach, was a Meafure of Policy, fuggefted by the firft Principles of Warfare, and led to repeated Attempts of this Kind during the Courfe of this Seafon.

On the 30th of Auguft it was reported in the Gazette fo often quoted in thefe Pages, that "General Wafhington, the Marquis de La Fayette, Generals Green and

Wayne, with many other Officers, and a large Body of Rebels, have been in the Vicinity of Bergen for some Time past. They have taken all the Forage from the Inhabitants of that Place, and left them destitute of every Thing for their present and Winter Subsistence. Their Officers were down as low as Prior's Mills last Friday, but did not seem inclined to make any Attack. Their Artillery, save some few Pieces, with their Baggage, are about twenty Miles in the Country."

Several separate Editions of *The Cow Chace* has been published, and it has often appeared in the Columns of Periodicals, and in Collections of Poems relating to this Period.

As a Specimen of Literature, while it has some Faults, it has other Points of great Beauty, and it everywhere bears Evidence that its Author possessed a keen Sense of the Ludicrous, and the Ability to seize upon those Points of his Subject which allowed the best Opportunity for its Exercise.

## Preface.

We have thought proper to infert as an Introduction to the Poem, the Preface and Advertifement of the London Edition of 1781, and fuch Letters and Newfpaper Articles, as might moft fully prefent the Reports of both Sides upon the Subject, with many little Incidents that further ferve to give it Intereft. The Bitternefs of partizan Feeling which fo largely influenced the Statements and Opinions of Cotemporaries, has long fince paft into Oblivion, and no one will at this Day, cherifh the Memory of our illuftrious Wafhington, and his diftinguifhed Companions in Arms with lefs Veneration, by knowing what was faid againft them by Partizans within the Enemy's Lines, who had every Motive for weakening their Influence, and throwing Ridicule upon their Acts.

# INTRODUCTION.

*Advertisement of the London Edition.*\*

THE following Poem was written by the late gallant MAJOR ANDRE, who was condemned to die *for doing his Duty* to his King and Country, by a Set of Miscreants, calling themselves "*General Officers*" in the American *Rebellion*; all of whom are a thousand Times more deserving of Death for their *Crimes*, with the inhuman

---

\* The | Cow Chace : | an | Heroick Poem in three Cantos, | Written at New York, 1780. | By the late Major André, | with Explanatory Notes, by the Editor. |

> " The Man who fights, and runs away,
> " May live to fight another day,"
> Said Butler in his deathless lay :
>
> " But he who is in battle slain,
> " Can never rise to fight again ;"
> As wisely thought good General Wayne.

London : | Printed for John Fielding, No. 23 Pater-Noster-Row, 1781. | 4to, pp. 32.

*Washington* at their Head, by whose Authority their Sentence was put into execution, and who has, by his own personal Orders, caused more than *fifteen hundred* British Subjects to be executed since he became a *Traitor*, for the bare Profession of *Loyalty*, and because they would not add, as *he* had done, *Perjury* and *Treason* to *Cruelty* and *Rapine*. Yet are there even *Britons* so lost to Shame, and so dead to Humanity, as to applaud his Conduct.

### Preface of the London Edition, 1781.

THE Poem is founded on the Defeat of the Rebel Generals, Wayne, Irving, and Procter, by a small Body of Refugees, as stated in the following Gazettes. The principal Subject is the taking and retaking of the Cattle; that Part of the Story affording the best Opportunity for Humour.

The last Stanza must awaken the Sensibility of the Reader. It seems to have been prophetic of the disastrous Fate of the ac-

*Introduction.*

complished Author. The Poem was printed in separate Cantos at New York; the last Canto on the very Day the Major was taken Prisoner.

*Letter from General Washington to the President of Congress.*

[From the Pennsylvania Packet, August 1, 1780.]

HEAD QUARTERS, (Bergen County) July 26, 1780.

SIR,

Having received Information that there were considerable Numbers of Cattle and Horses on Bergen Neck, within Reach of the Enemy, and having Reason to suspect that they meant shortly to draw all Supplies of that Kind within their Lines, I detached Brigadier General Wayne, on the 20th, with the first and second Pennsylvania Brigades, with four Pieces of Artillery attached to them, and Colonel Moyland's\* Regiment of Dragoons to bring them off. I had it also in Contemplation to attempt at the

\* Stephen Moylan.

same Time, the Destruction of a Blockhouse at Bull's Ferry,* which served the Purpose of covering the Enemy's Woodcutters, and giving Security to a Body of Refugees, by whom it was garrisoned, and who committed Depredations upon the well-affected Inhabitants for many Miles round.

General Wayne having disposed of his Troops in such a Manner as to guard the different Landing Places on the Bergen Shore, upon which the Enemy might throw over Troops from York Island to intercept his Retreat, and having sent down his Cavalry to execute the Business of driving off the Stock, proceeded with the first, second and tenth Regiments, and the Artillery, to

---

* Bull's Ferry is a Landing and Hamlet at the Foot of the Palisades on the New Jersey Shore, opposite 90th Street New York City. A Steam Ferry now connects it with the City. It is the Seat of a Post Office of this Name.

Blockhouse Point is a short Distance below, and derives its Name from the Blockhouse that was the Scene of Events described in Andre's Poem. The Place was named from a Family who were living there at the Time of the Attack.

## Introduction. 13

the Block-house, which he found surrounded by an Abatis and Stockade. He for some Time, tried the Effect of his Field Pieces upon it, but tho' the Fire was kept up for an Hour, they were found too light to penetrate the Logs of which it was constructed. The Troops during this Time, being galled by a constant Fire from the Loop-holes of the House, and seeing no Chance of making a Breach with Cannon, the first and second Regiments, notwithstanding the utmost Efforts of the Officers to restrain them, rushed through the Abatis to the Foot of the Stockade, with a View of forcing an Entrance, which was found impracticable.

This Act of intemperate Valour, was the Cause of the Losses sustained, and which amounted in the whole, to three Officers wounded, 15 non-commissioned and Privates killed, and 46 non-commissioned and Privates wounded. The wounded Officers are, Lieutenants Hammond and Crawford, of the first, and Lieutenant De Hart, of the second, the last since dead. I cannot but mention his Death with Regret, as he was a young Gentleman of amiable Qualities, and who promised fair to be servicable to his Country.

The Dragoons, in the mean Time, drove off the Stock which were found on the Neck; the Sloops and Wood boats in the Dock near the Block-house were burnt, and a few People on board them made Prisoners.

I have been thus particular, lest the Accounts of this Affair should have reached Philadelphia much exaggerated, as is commonly the Case on such Occasions.

  I have the honour to be,
   With the greatest respect, Sir,
    Your Excellency's most
     Obedient Servant,
      GEORGE WASHINGTON.

His Excellency *Samuel Huntington*, Esquire.

  Published by Order of Congress.
   *Charles Thompson*, Sec'y.

*Introduction.*

### Newspaper Notices.

[From Rivington's Royal Gazette, No. 398, July 22, 1780.]

> Jonathan these Babes of thine,
> Are not all Children genuine.

Yesterday Morning about nine o'Clock, Generals Wayne and Irwin, with the 1st and 2d Pennsylvania Brigades of Infantry, Colonel Moylan's Cavalry, and Proctor's* Artillery, the Flower of Washington's Army, consisting of about 1800 Troops, with 6 six Pounders, and one Howitzer, appeared in View of Col. Cuyler's Refugee Post, on the Jersey Shore, which was then commanded by Captain Thomas Ward; about ten o'Clock they advanced with their Cannon, within one hundred and sixty Yards of the Refugee Works, and commenced a tremendous Cannonade, which lasted till half past eleven. They attempted

---

\* Col. Thomas Proctor was a Native of Ireland, and settled in America before the Revolution. By Trade he was a Carpenter. He died at Philadelphia, March 16, 1807, aged 67 Years, and his Remains were interred in St. Paul's Church Yard in that City.

to ftorm the Abatis, but were repulfed with the Lofs of about ninety killed and wounded, among which are five Officers. The Lofs of the Refugees, is four killed and eight flightly wounded. No Veterans could have behaved better than thefe few Loyalifts; and his Excellency the Commander in Chief, has expreffed his Thanks and Approbation, to this LOYAL BAND, for their fpirited and gallant Behaviour.

[From Rivington's Royal Gazette, No. 399, July 26, 1780.]

The following are the Names of the brave Refugees that were killed and wounded at Colonel Cuyler's Refugee Poft, near Fort Lee, on Hudfon's River, on Friday the 21ft Inft. (as mentioned in our laft,) viz. Thomas Philips, of the Artillery, John McMurdy, with another Man and a Negro killed.

Lieutenants George and Abfalom Bull, Alexander Sharp, John and Ezekiel Fealy, and John Mullan wounded.

*Introduction.* 17

The principal Rebel Officers on the Attack, were Colonels Moylan, Stewart, Hays, Proctor, and the Majors Lee* and More.

Thus the chosen Band of Washington's Army, were repulsed by a few determined Loyalists; and we have Reason to believe the Loss of the Rebels much greater than has yet been ascertained; and to add more to the Spirit of the Refugees, a Party under the Command of the brave Captain Ward, pursued the Rear of the retreating Army upwards of four Miles, retook twenty Head of Cattle that were carried off from the well affected Neighbourhood, killed one Rebel, and made Prisoner of General Wayne's Servant and another.

*The following Approbation was signified to Colonel Cuyler, by the Adjutant General.*

Head Quarters, July 21, 1780.

Sir, The Commander in Chief admiring

---

\* Major Henry Lee, afterwards a General in the Service, and Governor of Virginia. He was the Father of Robert E. Lee, Commander in Chief of the Rebel Armies, in the War of 1861-5.

the Gallantry of the Refugees, who in such small Numbers, defended their Post against so very considerable a Corps, and withstood both their Cannon and Assault, desires his very particular Acknowledgement of their Merit may be testified to them.

His Excellency requests you will give in a Return of the Numbers present at this spirited Defence, that he may give Directions for uniform Cloathing and Hats being given them from the Inspector General's Office.

In Future, *your* Requisition of Ammunition will be valid with the Ordnance.

  I have the the honour to be,
   Sir, your most obedient,
    and most humble Servant,
     JOHN ANDRE, A. D. G.

[Quoted in Rivington's Royal Gazette, No. 400, July 29, 1780.]

NEW-JERSEY.

"Chatham, July 26. Last Friday, General Wayne, with a Detachment of 1800 Men,

*Introduction.* 19

made an Aſſault upon a Blockhouſe of the Enemy near Bull's Ferry, on the North River, but finding it very ſtrong, (*held by only 84 Refugees*) drew off the Men. Our Loſs we are told, amounts to near 50 Killed and Wounded." (*But the Returns ſay* 150.)

*Card in Rivington's Gazette, July* 29, 1780.

" A Lady preſents her Compliments to the Sir Clement of Philadelphia Ball Room, and deſires the next Country Dances may commence with a new Movement, called,

A TRIP TO THE BLOCKHOUSE,
OR THE
WOOD CUTTERS TRIUMPH,

In Compliment to a certain General, who (emulating his Brother *Arnold,*) was lately checked on the North River, by a *Malheureuſe* Event, and his Glories (now on the *Wane*) threatened with an inſuperable Mortification."

(Publifhed by Authority.)

*Extract of a Letter from Sir* HENRY CLINTON *to Lord* GEORGE GERMAIN, *dated Eaft Hampton, Suffolk County, Long Ifland, Auguft* 20, 1780.

[From the London Gazette.]

I have the Satisfaction of communicating to your Lordfhip an Inftance of Courage, which reflects the greateft Honour on a fmall Body of the Refugees.

About *feventy* of them had taken Poft on a Part of the oppofite Shore on the North River, called Bull's Ferry, where they had fortified themfelves with a Block-houfe and Stockade, to be protected in cutting Wood, the Labour they were employed in for their Maintenance.

A Corps of near *two thoufand* Rebels, under their Generals Wayne, Irving and Proctor, with feven Pieces of Cannon, made an Attack upon them on the 21ft ult. Notwithftanding a Cannonade of three Hours, almost every Shot of which penetrated through the Block-house, and an Attempt to carry the Place by Assault, they were repulsed by these *brave Men*, with the Loss of a great many killed and wounded. The Exertions of the Refugees did not cease: after having resisted so great a Force, they followed the Enemy, seized their Stragglers, and *rescued from them the Cattle they were driving from the neighbouring District*.

The Block-house which I visited, was pierced with fifty-two Shot in one Face only, and the small Guns that were in it were dismounted. Six of the Refugees were killed and fifteen wounded,—the far greater Part in the Block-house.[*]

[*] It is highly probable, that Major Andre accompanied General Clinton on this Visit to the Blockhouse.

22        *Introduction.*

[From Rivington's Royal Gazette, No. 439, December 13, 1780.]

HEAD QUARTERS, 11th Dec., 1780.

Sir, I have the Pleasure of sending you, by the Direction of his Excellency the Commander in Chief, the enclosed Extract of a Letter which he has received by the last Pacquet, from Lord George Germain, one of his Majesty's principal Secretaries of State, and which he is happy to communicate to you by the first Opportunity.

I am, Sir, your most obedient
humble Servant,

FRED. MACKENZIE, D. A. Gen.

Capt. Ward,* Loyal Refugees.

---

* Capt. Thomas Ward, was from Newark, New Jersey, and had originally sided with the Whig Party. He was the Leader of a Band of Outlaws, and plundered wherever he found Opportunity.—*Sabine's Loyalists*, i, 400.

Ward was subsequently transferred to a Block House at Bergen Point, where on the 7th of October, he was again attacked by a Party of Infantry and Horse, reported by British Accounts as two hundred strong, and succeeded in resisting them. On the 21st of November he attempted to surprise the American Guard at Newark and was repulsed.

*Introduction.* 23

*Extract of a Letter from Lord* George Germain, *to his Excellency, Sir* Henry Clinton, *dated 4th October,* 1780.

" The very extraordinary Inftance of Courage fhewn by the Loyal Refugees, in the Affair of Bull's Ferry, of which you make fuch honourable Mention, is a pleafing Proof of the Spirit and Refolution with which Men in their Circumftances will act againft their Oppreffors, and how great Advantage the King's Troops may derive from employing thofe of approved Fidelity. And his Majefty, to encourage fuch Exertions, commands me to defire you will acquaint the Survivors of the brave Seventy, that their intrepid Behaviour is approved of by their Sovereign."

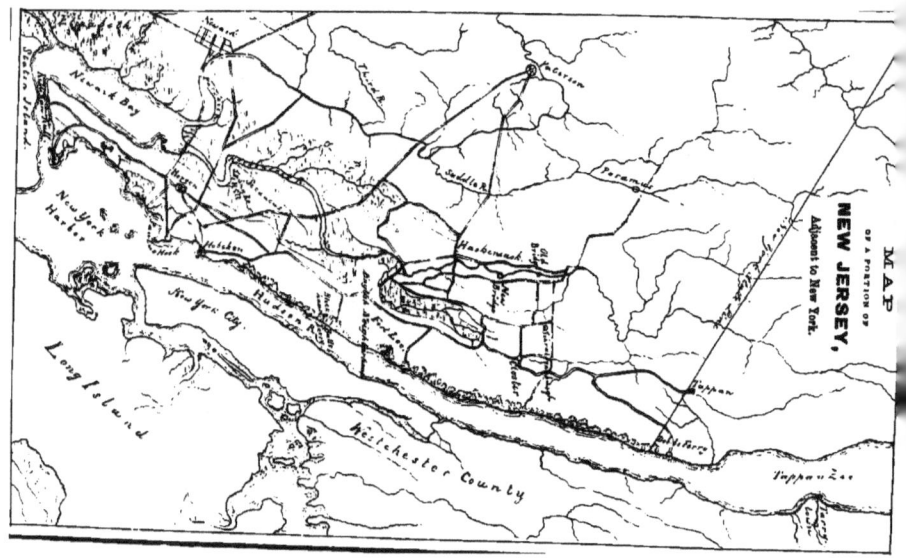

# THE
# COW CHACE.*

### Canto I.[1]

TO drive the Kine, one Summer's Morn,
    The Tanner[2] took his Way,—
The Calf shall rue that is unborn
    The Jumbling of that Day.

And Wayne descending Steers shall know,
    And tauntingly deride,
And call to Mind in ev'ry *Low*,
    The Tanning of *his* Hide.

---

\* The References by Figures, are to corresponding Numbers in the Notes at the End of the Poem.

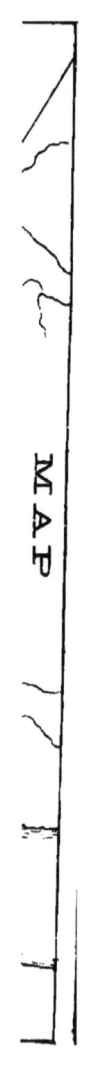

THE

# COW CHACE.*

### Canto I.[1]

TO drive the Kine, one Summer's Morn,
　The Tanner[2] took his Way,—
The Calf shall rue that is unborn
　The Jumbling of that Day.

And Wayne descending Steers shall know,
　And tauntingly deride,
And call to Mind in ev'ry *Low*,
　The Tanning of *his* Hide.

\* The References by Figures, are to corresponding Numbers in the Notes at the End of the Poem.

Yet Bergen Cows ſtill ruminate
    Unconſcious in the ſtall,
What mighty Means were uſed to get
    And loſe them after all.

For many Heroes bold and brave
    From New-Bridge[3] and Tapaan,[4]
And thoſe that drink Paſſaick's[5] Wave,
    And thoſe that eat Soupaan.[6]

And Sons of diſtant Delaware
    And ſtill remoter Shannon,[7]
And Major Lee[8] with Horſes rare
    And Procter[9] with his Cannon.

All wond'rous proud in Arms they came
    What Hero could refuſe?
To tread the rugged Path to Fame
    Who had a Pair of Shoes.[10]

## The Cow Chace.

At *six* the Hoſt with ſweating Buff,
   Arriv'd at Freedom's Pole,[11]    [enough
When Wayne, who thought he'd Time
   Thus ſpeechified the Whole:

" O ye whom Glory doth unite
   " Who Freedom's Cauſe eſpouſe
" Whether the Wing that's doom'd to fight
   " Or that to *drive the Cows:*

" 'Ere yet you tempt your further Way
   " Or into Action come,
" Hear Soldiers what I have to ſay
   " And take a Pint of Rum.

" Intemp'rate Valour then will ſtring,
   " Each nervous Arm the better
" So all the Land ſhall IO ſing
   " And read the Gen'ral's Letter.[12]

" Know that fome paltry Refugees
  " Whom I've a Mind to fight,
" Are playing H—l amongft the Trees,
  " That grow on yonder Height.

" Their Fort and Block Houfes we'll level,
  " And deal a horrid Slaughter,
" We'll drive the Scoundrels to the Devil
  " And ravifh Wife and Daughter.

" I, under Cover of th' Attack
  " Whilft you are all at Blows,
" From Englifh Neighb'rood[13] and Tinack[14]
  " Will *drive away* the *Cows*.

" For well you know the latter is
  " The ferious Operation
" And fighting with the Refugees
  " Is only Demonftration."

His daring Words from all the Crowd
   Such great Applause did gain
That every Man declar'd aloud
   For *serious Work* with Wayne.

Then from the Cask of Rum once more
   They took a heady Jill,
When one and all they loudly swore
   They'd fight upon the Hill.

But here—the Muse has not a Strain
   Befitting such great Deeds,
Huzza they cried, huzza for Wayne
   And shouting—did their Needs.

*End of Canto the First.*

THE

# COW CHACE.

### Canto II.[15]

NEAR his meridian Pomp the Sun
    Had journey'd from the Horizon,
When fierce the dusky Tribe mov'd on
    Of Heroes drunk as Poison.

The Sounds confus'd of boasting Oaths,
    Reecho'd thro' the Wood,
Some vow'd to sleep in dead Men's Cloaths,
    And some to swim in Blood.

At Irvine's Nod 'twas fine to fee,
  The *Left* prepare to fight,
The while the Drovers, Wayne and Lee,
  Drew off upon the *Right*.

Which Irvine 'twas, Fame don't relate,
  Nor can the Mufe affift her,
Whether 'twas he that cocks a Hat,
  Or he that gives a Glifter.[16]

For greatly one was fignaliz'd
  That fought at Chefnut-Hill,
And Canada immortaliz'd,
  The Vender of the Pill.

Yet the Attendance upon Procter,
  They both might have to boaft of;
For there was Bufinefs for the Doctor,
  And Hatts to be difpof'd of.

Let none uncandidly infer,
  That Stirling wanted Spunk,
The felf-made Peer had fure been there,
  But that the Peer was drunk.

But turn we to the Hudfon's Banks,
  Where ftood the modeft Train,
With Purpofe firm, tho' flender Ranks,
  Nor car'd a Pin for Wayne.

For them the unrelenting Hand
  Of Rebel Fury drove,
And tore from ev'ry genial Band,
  Of Friendfhip and of Love.

And fome within a dungeon's Gloom,
  By mock Tribunals laid,
Had waited long a cruel Doom,
  Impending o'er their Heads.

Here, one bewails a Brother's Fate,
  There one a Sire demands,
Cut off, alas! before their Date
  By ignominious Hands.

And silver'd Grandsires here appear'd,
  In deep Distress serene,
Of reverend Manners, that declar'd,
  That better Days they'd seen.

Oh curs'd Rebellion these are thine
  Thine all these Tales of Woe,
Shall at thy dire insatiate Shrine
  Blood never cease to flow?

And now the Foe began to lead
  His Forces to th' Attack;
Balls whistling unto Balls succeed,
  And made the Block-house crack.

## The Cow Chace.

No Shot could pafs, if you will take
  The Gen'ral's Word for true;[17]
But 'tis a d——ble Miftake,
  For every Shot went thro'.

The firmer as the Rebels prefs'd,
  The loyal Heroes ftand;
Virtue had nerv'd each honeft Breaft,
  And Induftry each Hand.

" In valour's Phrenzy,* Hamilton
  " Rode like a Soldier big,
" And Secretary Harrifon,[19]
  " With Pen ftuck in his Wig.

" But leaft their Chieftain Wafhington,
  " Should mourn them in the Mumps,†

\* Vide Lee's Trial. (See Note 18.)
† A Diforder prevalent in the Rebel Lines. (See Note 20.)

## The Cow Chace.

" The Fate of Withrington to fhun,
  " Thought *behind* the Stumps."\*

But ah, Thadæus Poffet, why
  Should thy poor Soul elope,
And why fhould Titus Hooper die,
  Ah die—without a Rope!

Apoftate Murphy, thou to whom
  Fair Shela ne'er was cruel,
*In Death fhalt hear her* mourn thy Doom,
  " Auch wou'd you die my Jewel?"

Thee, Nathan Pumpkin I lament,
  Of melancholy Fate,
The Grey Goofe ftolen as he went,
  In his Heart's Blood was wet.[22]

---

\* " The Merit of thefe Lines, which is doubtlefs very great, can
" only be felt by true Connoiffeures converfant in antient Song."
(See Note 21.)

Now as the Fight was further fought,
　　And Balls began to thicken,
The Fray aſſum'd, the Gen'rals thought,
　　The Colour of a Licking.

Yet undiſmay'd the Chiefs command,
　　And to redeem the Day,
Cry, *Soldiers, charge!* they hear, they ſtand,
　　They turn, and run away.

*End of Canto the Second.*

THE

# COW CHACE.

### Canto III.[23]

NOT all delights the bloody Spear,
  Or horrid Din of Battle,
There are, I'm sure, who'd like to hear
  A Word about the Cattle.

The Chief whom we beheld of late,
  Near Schralenburgh[24] haranguing,
At Yan Van Poop's,[25] unconscious sat
  Of Irving's hearty Banging.

Whilst valiant Lee, with Courage wild,
  Most bravely did oppose
The Tears of Woman and of Child,
  Who begg'd he'd leave the Cows.

But Wayne, of sympathising Heart,
  Required a Relief
Not all the Blessings could impart
  Of Battle or of Beef,

For now a Prey to female Charms,
  His Soul took more delight in
A lovely *Hamadryad's Arms,
  Than driving Cows or fighting;

A Nymph, the Refugees had drove
  Far from her native Tree,

* A Deity of the Woods.

## The Cow Chace.

Juft happen'd to be on the Move,
    When up came Wayne and Lee.

She in mad Anthony's fierce Eye
    The Hero faw pourtray'd,
And all in Tears fhe took him by
    —The Bridle of his Jade.[26]

" Hear, faid the Nymph, O great Com-
   " No *human* Lamentations;   [mander!
" The Trees you fee them cutting yonder
   " Are all my near Relations;

" And I, forlorn! implore thine Aid,
   " To free the facred Grove;
" So fhall thy Prowefs be repaid
   " With an Immortal's Love."

Now fome, to prove fhe was a Goddefs,
    Said this enchanting Fair

Had late retired from the *Bodies*,*
    In all the Pomp of War;

That Drums and merry Fifes had play'd
    To honour her Retreat,
And Cunningham²⁷ himself convey'd
    The Lady thro' the street.

Great Wayne, by soft Compassion sway'd,
    To no Enquiry stoops,
But takes the fair afflicted Maid
    *Right* into Yan Van Poop's.

So Roman Anthony, they say,
    Disgrac'd th' imperial Banner,
And for a Gipsy ²⁸ lost a Day,
    Like Anthony the Tanner.

    A cant Appellation given amongst the Soldiery to the Corps
that has the Honour to guard his Majesty's Person.

The Hamadryad had but half
    Receiv'd Redress from Wayne,
When Drums and Colours, Cow and Calf,
    Came down the Road amain.

All in a Cloud of Dust were seen
    The Sheep, the Horse, the Goat,
The gentle Heifer, Ass obscene,
    The Yearling, and the Shoat,

And Pack-horses with Fowls came by,
    Befeather'd on each Side,
Like Pegasus, the Horse that I
    And other Poets ride.

Sublime upon his Stirrups rose
    The mighty Lee behind,
And drove the terror-smitten Cows,
    Like Chaff before the Wind.

But fudden fee the Woods above
    Pour down another Corps,
All helter fkelter in a Drove,
    Like that I fung before.

Irving and Terror in the Van,
    Came flying all abroad,
And Cannon, Colours, Horfe and Man
    Ran tumbling to the Road.

Still as he fled, 'twas Irving's Cry,
    And his Example too,
" Run on, my merry Men all—For why?
" The Shot will not go thro'."\*

> \* Five Refugees ('tis true) were found
>     Stiff on the Blockhoufe floor,
> But then 'tis thought the Shot went round,
>     And in at the back Door.

As when two Kennels in the Street,
    Swell'd with a recent Rain,
In gushing Streams together meet,
    And seek the neighbouring Drain;

So met these dung-born Tribes in one,
    As swift in their Career,
And so to Newbridge they ran on,—
    But all the Cows got clear.

Poor Parson Caldwell,[29] all in Wonder,
    Saw the returning Train,
And mourn'd to Wayne the lack of Plunder,
    For them to steal again.

For 'twas his Right to seize the Spoil, and
    To Share with each Commander
As he had done at Staten Island,
    With frost-bit Alexander.[30]

In his Difmay the frantick Prieft
  Began to grow prophetic,
You'd fwore, to fee his lab'ring Breaft,
  He'd taken an Emetic.

" I view a future Day," faid he,
  " Brighter than this Day dark is,
" And you fhall fee what you fhall fee,—
  " Ha! ha! one pretty Marquis.[31]

" And he fhall come to Paulus Hook,[32]
  " And great Atchievements *think* on,
" And make a Bow, and take a Look,
  " Like Satan over Lincoln.

" And all the Land around fhall glory
  " To fee the Frenchmen caper,
" And pretty Sufan[33] tell the Story
  " In the next Chatham Paper."

## The Cow Chace.

This solemn Prophecy, of course,
  Gave all much Consolation,
Except to Wayne, who lost his Horse
  Upon the *great* Occasion.

His Horse that carried all his Prog,
  His military Speeches,
His corn-stalk Whisky for his Grog,
  Blue Stockings, and brown Breeches.

And now I've clos'd my epic Strain,
  And tremble as I shew it,
Lest this same Warrio-drover, Wayne,
  Should ever catch the Poet.[34]

*F I N I S.*

# NOTES.

### Note 1, Page 25.

This Canto was first printed in Rivington's *Royal Gazette*, No. 405, August 16, 1780.

### Note 2, Page 25.

Wayne's legal Occupation.—*Note in London Edition.*
Before entering the Service Wayne was a Land Surveyor.

### Note 3, Page 26.

New-Bridge, a Hamlet in Bergen County, N. J., about fourteen Miles northwest of Jersey City.

### Note 4, Page 26.

Tappan was within the present Limits of Orangetown, Rockland County, N. Y. This was the Scene of André's Trial and Execution, a few Weeks after this Canto was written.

### Note 5, Page 26.

A River in New Jersey.—*Note in London Edition.*

### Note 6, Page 26.

Hasty Pudding made of the Meal of Indian Corn.—*Note in London Edition.*

### Note 7, Page 26.

The Number of Irish in the Pennsylvania Line often caused it to be called in the War the Line of Ireland.—*Sargent's Life of André*, 237.

### Note 8, Page 26.

Major Henry Lee of the Dragoons.

### Note 9, Page 26.

Captain Thomas Proctor.

### Note 10, Page 26.

"They are of a thin long-legged Make, most of them without Shoes and Stockings, and without Coats, and sometimes they throw away their Arms when they are close pursued." MS. *Mather's Journal*, quoted by Mr. Sargent, in his *Life of André*, p. 237.

### Note 11, Page 27.

"Freedom's—*i. e.* Liberty Pole—a long Tree stuck in the Ground."—*Note in London Edition.* Its Place was between Orangetown and Tinack.—*Sargent's André*, 237.

### Note 12, Page 27.

Mr. Sargent suggests that this may have been the Letter of General Washington, dated July 26, 1780, and printed on Page 12 of this Volume.—*Sargent's André*, 238.

### Note 13, Page 28.

English Neighborhood, a Settlement in New Jersey, then within the American Lines.

## Notes.

### Note 14, Page 28.

Tinack, a Hamlet in Bergen County, New Jersey.

### Note 15, Page 30.

This Canto was first published in Rivington's *Royal Gazette*, No. 409, August 30, 1780.

### Note 16, Page 31.

One of the Irvines was a Hatter and the other a Physician.—*Note in London Edition.* Dr. William Irvine, after two Years' Captivity in Canada, now commanded the 2d Pennsylvania Regiment. Brigadier James Irvine of the Militia, it will be recollected, was taken at Chestnut Hill, December 1777.—*Sargent's André*, 240.

### Note 17, Page 33.

"So Washington wrote to the Congress; a body of Men at first of some Reputation, but now consisting only of Bankrupts and Knaves,—always excepting the renowned JOHNY WITHERSPOON, who is perfectly adapted to his Situation; concerning whom it may be useful to observe, that it has not yet been settled which of the three he is most fond of,—Heresy, Sedition, or Strong Toddy: Perhaps he may be best suited by the Bath Motto, TRIA JUNCTA IN UNO."—*Note in London Edition.*

### Note 18, Page 34.

Wayne attributed his Failure to the Lightness of his Pieces, which he thought made no Impression upon the Walls of the House. In this he was probably mistaken.—*Sparks's Washington*, vii, 117.

### Note 19, Page 34.

" When General Washington asked me if I would remain in Front, and retain the Command, or he should take it, and I had answered that I undoubtedly would, and that he should see that I myself should be one of the last to leave the Field; Colonel Hamilton flourishing his Sword immediately exclaimed—that's right, my dear General, and I will stay, and we will all die here on this Spot. I could not but be surprised at his Expression, but observing him much fluttered and in a sort of *Phrenzy of Valour*, I calmly requested him to observe me well, and tell me if I did not appear tranquil and Master of my Faculties: his Answer was, that he must own that I was entirely possessed of myself: Well then (said I,) you must allow me to be a proper Judge of what I ought to do."—*Gen. Chas. Lee's Trial*, p. 129, ed. of 1823.

### Note 20, Page 34.

Col. Robert H. Harrison. Major André with Col. West Hyde had met Col. Harrison and Col. William Davies at Amboy in May, 1779, to endeavor to negotiate an Exchange of Prisoners. They remained from the 12th to the 23d and effected nothing.—*Sargent's André*, 217.

### Note 21, Page 35.

" For Witherington needs must I wayle
    As one in doleful Dumps;
For when his Legges were smitten off,
    He fought upon his Stumpes."—*Chevy Chace*.

## Notes.

### Note 22, Page 35.

" Againſt Sir Hugh Montgomery
So right the Shaft he fett,
The grey Goofe-wing that was thereon
In his Heart's blood was wett."—*Chevy Chafe*.

### Note 23, Page 37.

This Canto was firſt printed in Rivington's *Royal Gazette*, No. 416, September 24, 1780.

### Note 24, Page 37.

Schralenberg, a Village in Bergen County, N. J., five Miles Northeaſt of Hackenfac.

### Note 25, Page 37.

"Who kept a Dram-Shop."—*Note in London Edition*.

### Note 26, Page 39.

A New England Name for a Horfe, Mare, or Gelding.—*Note in London Edition*.

### Note 27, Page 40.

That is, the Lady had been drummed out of the Lines as a common Drunkard or Thief: Cunningham was the Provoſt Marſhal. "There are a Number of Women here of bad Charaćter, who are continually running to New York, and back again. If they were Men, I would flog them without Mercy." A. Burr, commanding on American Lines in Weſtcheſter County, to Gen. McDougall; White Plains, Jan. 21, 1779.—*Sargent's André*, 245.

### Note 28, Page 40.

Cleopatra, Queen of Egypt.—*Note in London Edition*.

### Note 29, Page 42.

"Caldwell, a diffenting Minifter at Elizabeth Town, appointed Quarter-mafter General to the Rebel Army, and afterwards difmiffed for Embezzlement."—*Note in London Edition.*

Rev. James Caldwell of New Jerfey, an active Whig and Deputy Quarter-Mafter General, whofe Wife was barbaroufly fhot by a newly enlifted Soldier of Knyphaufen's command in the preceding Summer, on no other Provocation, as was alleged, than that fhe vituperated him from her Window as he paffed.

The Britifh were at this Time on an Expedition into the Interior of New Jerfey, to favor an Uprifing of Loyalifts which they had been led to believe needed only the Prefence of an armed Force for its Development. The invading Force confifted of five thoufand Men, and advanced to Springfield, and General Wafhington marched to the Short Hills in the Rear of that Place to await an Action. The Information which had been given, as to the favorable Temper of the Inhabitants however proved altogether unfounded, and the Britifh Army returned to the Place of their Landing without effecting any thing. It was followed and harraffed by the Americans, and fome Lofs occurred on both Sides.

The *New Jerfey Gazette*, of June 21ft, 1780, mentions the Murder of Mrs. Caldwell as follows:

\* \* "As foon as they came to Connecticut Farms, feven Miles from the Place of their landing, they began the Exercife of their awful Cruelty. Although they obferved great Difcipline and Decorum in Elizabethtown, yet at the Farms every Step was marked with wanton Cruelty and caufelefs Devaftations. They fet Fire to and utterly deftroyed the Prefbyterian Church, and fourteen Dwelling Houfes and Barns, fo that there are but two

## Notes.

Dwelling-houses remaining in that fertile Settlement. But Alas! this is only one Part of the horrid Scene.

In the Neighborhood lived the Rev. James Caldwell, whose Zeal and Activity in the Cause of his Country had rendered him an Object worthy of the Enemy's keenest Resentment. His Vigilance and Attention had always evaded every Attempt to injure him, and therefore it was now determined to wound him in an unguarded Part. Following the absurd Principles of too many of our incautious Countrymen he left his Wife and Family at Home, trusting to the Politeness and Humanity of the Enemy towards an amiable Woman, and a Number of helpless and innocent Children, though he did not think it prudent to trust them with his own Safety. He had been warned of their utmost Hatred of him, and therefore dissuaded from leaving his Family in their Power; but, alas! his Confidence in their Benevolence towards the Helpless, has been his Destruction.

Soon after possessing themselves of the Neighborhood, a Soldier came to the House, and putting his Gun to the Window of the Room where this worthy Woman was sitting, (with her Children, and a Maid with an Infant in her Arms, alongside of her), he shot her through the Lungs dead on the Spot. Soon after an Officer with the Hessians came in and ordered a Hole dug and her Body thrown in, and the House to be set on Fire. At the earnest Request of an Officer of the new Levies, and with some Difficulty, the Body was suffered to be carried to a small House in the Neighborhood, and Mr. Caldwell's Dwelling was immediately set on fire, and every thing belonging to him consumed together. The only Comfort arising to this afflicted Family is, that the Wretch who served as the Executioner of this murdered Lady (who, from her excellent Character, deserved a better Fate), did his Business so effectually that she lost her Life without Dif-

tress or Pain. Thus it is, that even the tender Mercies of the
Wicked are Cruelty. This Melancholy Affair, with their cruel
Burnings, has raised the Resentment of the whole Country to the
highest Pitch. They are ready almost to swear an everlasting
Enmity to the very Name of Briton. So far is this Cruelty and
Devastation from terrifying them to Submission, that it rouses the
most Timid to Feats of desperate Heroism. A most worthy Man,
who has for four Years past, devoted himself to the Service of his
Country, is thus left with nine small Children, destitute even of a
Shift of Clothes to comfort them. Many of the Inhabitants are
in a similar Situation; some Widows, some Aged, some Infirm."

Chief Justice Marshall in alluding to this Incursion says:

"At the Connecticut Farms, a flourishing Settlement which
took its Name from the Country of those by whom it had been
planted, and which had been distinguished for its Zeal in the
American Cause, a Halt was made. In a Spirit of Revenge un-
worthy the General of an Army, which was in the Character of
Tryon, who was present, rather than of Knyphausen who commanded; which served to injure more than advance the Interests
of those in whose Cause he was engaged; and tended more to
irritate than intimidate; this Settlement including the Meeting-
house and the House of the Clergyman belonging to the Village,
was reduced to Ashes."

In a Note, he adds:

"This Circumstance would scarcely have deserved Notice, had
it not been accompanied by one of those melancholy Events,
which even War does not authorize, and which the civilized
World condemns, and which made at the Time a very deep
Impression.

"Mrs. Caldwell the Wife of the Clergyman, who has been
mentioned, had been induced to remain in her House, under the

## Notes. 55

Perfuafion that her Prefence might ferve to protect it from Pillage, and that her Perfon could not poffibly be endangered, as in the Hope of preferving the Farms, Colonel Dayton who at that Time commanded the Militia, determined not to halt in the Settlement, but to take Poft at a narrow Pafs on the Road leading to Springfield. While fhe was fitting in the Midft of her Children, having a fucking Infant in her Arms, a Soldier came up to the Window and difcharged his Mufket at her. She received the Ball in her Bofom, and inftantly expired.

Afhamed of an Act fo univerfally execrated, it was contended by the Britifh, that this Lady was the Victim of a random Shot, and even that the fatal Ball had proceeded from the Militia ; in Proof of which laft Affertion, they infifted that the Ball had entered on that Side which looked towards the retreating Americans. But it was Notorious that the Militia made no Stand at the Farms, and a pathetic Reprefentation of the Fact, made to the Public by the afflicted Hufband, received univerfal Credence and excited univerfal Indignation. The Death of Mrs. Caldwell, might indeed be confidered as the Act of a fingle Soldier, and therefore not involving the Reputation of the Army; but when with it was connected, the wanton and ufelefs Devaftation committed by Authority, thefe Acts formed one connected Whole in the public Mind, and ferved ftill more to confirm the fettled Hate of the well affected, againft the Britifh Government."—*Marfhall's Wafhington*, iv, 225.

To relieve the Britifh Caufe of the Odium which the Death of Mrs. Caldwell occafioned, a Loyalift named Fofter, who had probably followed the Britifh Army to affift in plundering, addreffed the following Letter to Rivington's Gazette, which was publifhed on the 5th of Auguft, 1780:

## Notes.

" To the Printer.

Sir, Agreeable to your Requeſt, I give the following Narrative of what I ſaw, heard and conceived relative to the Death of Mrs. Caldwell. Not, as you ſay, to contradict the Rebel Accounts (for they ſufficiently contradict one another), but for the Satisfaction of ſuch judicious Inquirers as wiſh to be informed.

I, without being requeſted by any one, or attached to any Detatchment of the Army, from mere Curioſity, marched from Elizabethtown with a Column of Britiſh Troops. I did not enquire, nor do I yet know who commanded them. The Column halted near a Houſe ſaid to be Mr. Caldwell's. I ſoon ſaw a Group of Soldiers in and about ſaid Houſe, and on my nearer Approach, heard ſome of them mention (rather piteouſly,) a Woman's being ſhot. As ſoon as the Crowd diſperſed, I entered the Houſe, and not without Difficulty, found her lying on her Back on a Bed that ſtood in a ſmall dark back Bed room, (for I don't recollect it had any Window,) tho' it had two. Doors that opened into other Apartments.

She was to Appearance dead, and had a Cloth careleſsly thrown over her Face, which I did not remove, but left her, expecting the Troops would ſoon march, when her Friends might take Care of her. Some Time after this, a Detachment moved near Rahway River, I followed, and did not return; in leſs than three Hours, when ſome Perſon who was near Mr. Caldwell's Houſe, told me the Woman was ſtripped, and thrown off the Bed, but that a Britiſh Officer's coming in, had prevented the Soldiers from carrying off her Cloaths. On entering the Houſe, I found her laying on her Face on the Floor beſide the Bed, and moſt of what Cloaths had been pulled off by her Side. I concluded ſhe had been taken off the Bed that the Bedding might be taken from under her.

## *Notes.*

As I came out of the House, I met at the Door, a Mr. Benjamin Dunn, a Refugee from Piscataway, (New Jersey,) who seemed sensibly touched with the humane Feelings of an informed Loyalist. He had not yet seen the Corpse, but desired me to shew her to him, I did so. We then examined every Circumstance in our Power, in order if possible, to discover the Cause of the Lady's Death, who by this Time we had heard was Mrs. Caldwell. We found that on Account of a Pantry that was building on the back Side of the House, a small Spot of Covering had been pulled off opposite to the Bed whereon the Lady sat. The only Ball we could discover that touched the House, was the one that killed her. It appeared to have come from a northern Direction (in the Course of the Rebel fire,) and passed between Joints of the plastered Wall. It seemed to have passed so far above the Bed as to have hit her above her Girdle, and its passing through her left Breast, I account for, by supposing her to have sat in a stooping Posture.

Mr. Dunn and myself, (for I cannot say which proposed it,) concluded to go to the nearest House, which we did, and asked the Woman to call some of the neighboring Women, and go to lay the Corpse out. This she declined, but said, she would send for Assistance, if we could get Help to remove her to her House, which was done; and at the Instance of Mr. W. Chandler, a Hessian Sentinel was set at the Door, while the Women performed their last kind Office to their Friend. At this House was a young Woman who said that she sat on the same Bed with Mrs. Caldwell at the Time she was shot by the Continental Troops. About two Hours after the Corpse was removed, Mr. Caldwell's House was set on fire.

I am Sir, Your most obedient Humble Servant,

EBENEZER FOSTER.

[Mr. Foster, (who gives the above Account of Mrs. Caldwell's Fate, was a Justice of Peace in the County of Middlesex in New Jersey,) is a Gentleman of great Integrity, and a very loyal Subject.]"—*Note by Rivington.*

Mr. Caldwell was himself killed by an American Soldier, Nov. 24, 1781—*Sargent's André,* 247.

A British Account of this Invasion into New Jersey is given in Rivington's *Royal Gazette,* No. 389, June 21, 1780, as follows:

OPERATIONS,
*Of the Royal Army in New Jersey.*
To Mr. Rivington.
ELIZABETHTOWN, June 20, 1780.

Sir, As the REBELS, agreeable to their usual Practice, have published many glaring Falsehoods relative to the late Movement into New Jersey, I have been induced, from a regard to Truth, to send you the following Account of our Operations, which I request you will publish in your Gazette tomorrow.

A BRITISH OFFICER.

On Tuesday Night, the 6th Inst., the Troops made their first Landing upon Elizabethtown Meadows, and were crossed over by Divisions in succession from Staten Island, with some light Artillery, taking their Route by Elizabethtown and Connecticut Farms, towards Springfield. Dayton's Regiment, receiving Intimation of our Approach, retired with Precipitation, as did also the Jersey Regiments which compose Maxwell's Brigade, from their Position near Camps; the Militia of the Country, although incapable of making any fixed Resistance, did their utmost to incommode the Troops upon their March, and collecting from different Quarters, they assembled in some Force in the Vicinity of Springfield, forming a Junction with the Jersey Brigade at that

## *Notes.*

Place, and it is said that in the Courfe of Wednefday the 7th Inft. they were fupported by another Brigade detached from Morris Town.

The Troops halted upon fome Heights beyond Connecticut Farms, where they were ordered to take Poft till fuch Time as the Remainder of the Artillery, the Provifions and the other Waggons, with the Corps which brought up the Rear, joined the Army. From this Circumftance it is probable, the Rebels conceived, that whatever might have been the original Plan, it was intended to penetrate no further. Increafing in Numbers, they ufed every Exertion in their Power, in flying Parties to fire upon the advanced Picquets, and during the Courfe of the Day, they made different Attacks upon a Body of Yagers, which was advanced upon the Springfield Road; this produced much firing upon both Sides.

During the Courfe of the Evening it is reported that Information was received from the Southward which rendered it expedient to defer the Object in Agitation, and about two Hours afterwards the Troops returned towards Elizabeth Town, without a Shot being fired, taking Poft upon the Heights near the Point.

On Thurfday the 8th Inft. the Rebels advanced in fome Force to Elizabeth Town, and made an Attack upon the 22d Regiment, which was pofted fome little Diftance in Front of the Line. This Regiment was ordered to fall back, and the Rebels conceiving it was the Rear Guard of the Army they advanced with fome Rapidity, but were foon checked, and retired with Precipitation.

The Lofs fuftained during the Courfe of this Service is inconfiderable, nor can that of the Rebels be determined, as they conceal it.

Whilft the Troops were advancing to Connecticut Farms, the

Rebels fired out of the Houses agreeable to their usual Practice, from which Circumstance, Mrs. Caldwell had the Misfortune to be Shot by a random Ball. What heightens the Singularity of this Lady's unhappy Fate, is, that upon Enquiry it appears beyond a Doubt, that the Shot was fired by the Rebels themselves, as it entered the Side of the House from their Direction, and lodged in the Wall nearest the Troops then advancing.

The Manner in which the Rebels aggravate this unfortunate Affair in their Publications, is of a Piece with their uniform Conduct, plausable, but fallacious, nor is it to be wondered at, if a Rebellion which originated in Falshood, is prosecuted with Deceit; a Soldiery received with Smiles one Moment, and the following Instant butchered, (for in a military View it merits no other Name,) by a Set of People, who by their Clothing and Appointments cannot be distinguished from the quiet Inhabitants of the Country, may well be supposed to be exasperated; nor need we be surprised at their using the Torch to Dwellings which they find hourly occupied by armed Men, who either want the Generosity or the Spirit to close the present unhappy Contest, by a manly, open, Soldier-like Decision; whatever may be the humane Wishes of the Commanders, human Nature at Times, steps over the Barrier of Discipline, and Men of Judgment and Candour, in the great Scale of political Reasoning, do not wonder at Occurrences, which their private Feelings shrink at. Such are the Effects of intestine Divisions; miserable is the Fate of that Country, which is the Theatre of such a Quarrel, and accursed is the Man, or the Set of Men, who from Motives of private Lucre, or inordinate Ambition, have fanned a Flame, which if they are willing, they are now perhaps unable to extinguish.

A BRITISH OFFICER.

"After the Rebels had plundered the Inhabitants of Staten Island, in their Descent last January, Lord Stirling (who commanded the Invaders) issued an Order directed to Parson Caldwell, for the collecting and restoring all the Property to the several owners."—*Rivington's Gazette*, July 19, 1780.

To prove that this Order was not obeyed, a Letter is published in which it appears that a considerable Amount of such Articles as Mattrasses, Blankets, &c., had been retained *for Family Use*, by some Persons connected with the Expedition.

### Note 30, Page 43.

Calling himself, because he was ordered not to do it, Earl of Stirling, though no Sterling Earl.—*Note in London Edition*.

The Allusion is here made to an Expedition undertaken to Staten Island, for the Purpose of surprising Skinner's new Corps, that had been undertaken by the Americans under Lord Stirling in the preceding January. It was not Successful and the thinly clothed party that composed the Expedition suffered from the intense Cold. It is said that five hundred Soldiers were Frostbitten. A few Prisoners were taken by the Enemy.

The following Account of this Expedition was published in *Rivington's Gazette*, January 19, 1780:

"On Friday Night, the 14th Instant, a large Detachment from the Rebel Army, consisting it is supposed of between 3 and 4000 Men, with six Pieces of Cannon, and two Howitzers, moved suddenly from the Neighbourhood of Morristown, and being, (as it is reported,) transported in *Sleighs* over the Ice, reached Staten Island before Day break in the Morning of the 18th, bending their March towards Decker's Ferry.

"Col. Buskirk commanding the 4th Battalion of Brigadier General Skinner's Brigade posted there, having received Intelligence of their Approach, judged it proper to retire towards Robison's Ferry, not being in Force fufficient to oppofe fo confiderable a Corps. The Rebels purfued their March, and before Noon, took Poft upon the Heights near the Redout, conftructed at the north End of the Ifland ; from their Pofition, cutting off the Communications betwixt the Corps hutted there, and the Troops at Richmond and the Flag Staff. They remained in this Situation till early in the Morning of the 16th, when they were obferved retiring from Staten Ifland, without attempting any thing. They burnt Decker's Houfe, and a very few fmall Veffels frozen in by the Ice at that Place. A fmall Detachment which harraffed their Rear, made a few Prifoners, feveral Deferters came to the Different Pofts during their Stay on the Ifland. They committed many Exceffes, plundering and diftreffing the Inhabitants. Sixteen Prifoners had already been fent to New York, and it is imagined there are others not yet arrived from Staten Ifland."

In Retaliation for this, a Detachment of Britifh Troops on the Night of January 25th, furprifed an American Poft at Elizabethtown, and took off thirty-four Officers and Privates, and feveral prominent Citizens.—*Rivington's Gazette*, Jan. 29, 1780.

### Note 31, Page 44.

" Marquis de la Fayette, a French Coxcomb, in the Rebel Service."—*Note in London Edition.*

### Note 32, Page 44.

" A fmall Head-land in Hudfon's River, oppofite to New York."—*Note in London Edition.* It is now in Jerfey City.

## Notes.

### Note 33, Page 44.

Mifs Sufannah Livingfton, Daughter of Governor William Livingfton of New Jerfey, who was fufpected of writing political Articles, in fome of which André had come in for a Share of Satire. Mifs Livingfton fubfequently married John Cleves Symmes, the Father-in-law of Prefident Harrifon.

At the Time of the Invafion of the Britifh to Springfield, the Refidence of Governor Livingfton was in the Hands of the Enemy but was guarded againft Injury. It was claimed to have been reported in Rivington's Paper, that while fome Britifh Officers were at the Houfe, one of them was prefented with a Rofe by this Lady, and that afterwards he was wounded by a Shot fired on the Premifes.

No Article of this Kind was however publifhed in that Paper, either on or near the Time alleged, but it led to the following Correfpondence:

[From the New Jerfey Journal, July 12, 1780.]

Mr. Rivington, according to his ufual Practice, has inferted in his Gazette of the 29th ult., under the Signature of one of my Sex, the groffeft Falfehoods, refpecting what happened to Col. Gordon, near Governor Livingfton's Houfe, that ever entered the Heart of Man, Almoft every Syllable of that Publication, is a moft villainous Lie. There was not a fingle Mufket fired from behind the Governor's Houfe, nor Fields, nor was it the Colonel that was wounded, who had the Rofe in the Morning, but a Colonel Woromb, an Heffian Officer, who afked Leave to pick one as he was on his Horfe. This, Mr. Printer, you may depend on as a Fact, and it is in the Power of Colonel Gordon, and Col. Woromb to confirm my Words.

I am your Humble Servant,

CLARINDA.

## Notes.

*Mr. Rivington presents his most respectful Compliments to* Clarinda, *and assures her he is perfectly innocent of the Charge respecting the* Rose, *and other Imputations in the above Address. He has not printed or published, directly or indirectly, a single Line upon the Subject, and he takes leave to add that no Lady will from his Performance, ever meet with Injury or Disgust.*

We Conjecture the following Reply may have been witten by Major André:

### CARD TO MR. RIVINGTON.

ROSALINDA presents her Compliments to Mr. Rivington, regretting that the Name of one of the Sex should be connected with *Terms*, so very unlike those used by the distinguished Part of the *Fair!* However his Zeal and Loyalty may urge him through *Mistake*, to be *poetical in his prose Productions occasionally*, the World at large must quit him, of having merited the unguarded Attack of the Clarinda of Chatham, he having been silent of late in what regards *La petite Guerre;* and wholly occupied by the tremendous Maneuvres of the grand Fleets of Spain, France, and Holland, the former of which he has given a good Account of *uncontradicted*, and 'tis hoped, God willing, will soon give a further good Account of the *Ally* next in Rotation for *Flagelation*.

Rosalinda is informed that the British Officer refused the Honour of the *Rose* by Clarinda, is so very grateful for the *Favour*, that he will not relinquish his Right to it, and for the *first* Time, and as 'tis said (he hopes the last Time in his Life) he brags of the *Lady's Favours!* Received on Horse back, in like Manner as the gallant Hessian *Partizan*, honored by the Sign Manual of the fair Clarinda! It is whispered, that on the Return from the Excursion, notwithstanding he wore the sweet Present next his left Breast, the Afternoon he received *another*, in the Vicinity of Mr.

## Notes.

William L———'s Houfe, tho' alfo very honourable, not near fo *agreeable* as that he had the Pleafure to receive at 4 o'Clock that Morning!

### Note 34, Page 45.

By a Remarkable Coincidence Major Andrè was arrefted on the fame Day that this Canto was publifhed in the *Royal Gazette*. He was probably preparing to leave for the American Lines when the Poem was written. Brigadier General Wayne was one of the Board of General Officers that fentenced Andrè to Death, and he doubtlefs witneffed his Execution.

According to Mr. Frank Moore, the following Lines were found under Andrè's Signature, to a manufcript Copy of this Poem :

> " And when the epic Strain was fung
> The Poet by the Neck was hung,
> And to his Coft he finds too late
> The dung-born Tribe decides his Fate."

# INDEX.

ADVERTISEMENT of London Edition, 9.
Alexander, Wm., Lord Stirling, 43.
André, Major John, 21, 50, 64, 65.
 Letter of, 17.
Arnold, General, 19.

BERGEN, 4, 6, 26.
 Bergen Neck, 11.
Bergen Point, 22.
Block House at Bull's Ferry, 3, 12, 19, 20, 21, 28, 33, 48.
Bull, Abfalom, wounded, 16.
Bull, George, wounded, 16.
Bull's Ferry, 12, 20, 23.
Burr, Aaron, 51.
Bufkirk, Col., 61.
Butler, Parody on, 9.

CALDWELL, Rev. James, 43, 52, 53, 61.
 Killed, 58.
Caldwell, Mrs. James, murdered, 52, 53, 54, 55, 56, 57, 58, 60.
Cattle, Attempt to take, 11, 17.
Chandler, W., 57.
Cheftnut Hill, 31.

Chevy Chafe quoted, 50, 51.
Clarinda, Letter by, 63.
 Reply to, 64.
Cleopatra, 51.
Clinton, Sir Henry, Letter from, 20.
Clothing to be iffued to Loyalifts, 18.
Complimentary Notice of Col. Cuyler, 17.
 of Capt. Ward, 23.
Connecticut Farms, 52, 54, 58, 59.
Country Dances, Suggeftion relative to, 19.
Cow Chace, a Poem, 25.
Crawford, Lieut., wounded, 13.
Cunningham, 40, 51.
Cuyler, Col., 3, 15, 16, 17.

DAYTON, Col. 55.
 Dayton's Regiment, 58.
Decker's Ferry, 61, 62.
De Hart, Lieut., killed, 13.
Delaware, 26.
Deftitution of American Army, 5.
Dunlap, Mr., quoted, 4.
Dunn, Benjamin, 57.

## Index.

EAST Hampton, L. I., 20.
  Englifh Neighborhood, 28, 48.
Elizabethtown, 52, 58, 59, 62.

FEALY, John and Ezekiel, wounded, 16.
Fort Lee, 16.
Fofter, Ebenezer, 55, 57, 58.
France, Fleets of, 64.
Freedom's Pole, 27.

GERMAIN, Lord, Letter to, 20.
  Letter from, 23.
Gordon, Col., 63.
Green, General, 5.

HAMADRYAD, 38, 41.
  Hamilton, Alexander, 34, 50.
Hammond, Lieut., wounded, 13.
Harrifon, Col. Robert H., 34, 50.
Harrifon, Prefident, 63.
Hats to be iffued to Loyalifts, 18.
Hays, Col., 17.
Holland, Fleets of, 64.
Hudfon, 32, 62.
Huntington, Stephen, 14.
Hyde, Col. Weft, 50.

INTRODUCTION, 9.
  Irvine, James, 49.
Irving, [or Irvine] Gen. William, 10, 15, 20, 31, 37, 42, 49.

JERSEY Brigade, 58.
  Jerfey City, 62.

KNYPHAUSEN, Gen., 52, 54.

LADY'S Card, and Compliments, 19.
La Fayette, Marquis de, 5, 44, 62.
Lee, Gen. Charles, 50.
Lee, Major Henry, 17, 26, 31, 39, 41, 48.
Lee, Gen. Robert E., 17.
Letter from Gen. Wafhington, 11.
  Gen. Henry Clinton, 20.
  Major André, 17.
Liberty Pole, 48.
Livingfton, Sufannah, 44, 63.
Livingfton, Gov. William, 63, 65.

McDOUGALL, Gen., 51.
  McKenzie, Frederick, 22.
McMurdy, John, killed, 16.
Marfhall, Chief Juftice, 54.
Maxwell's Brigade, 58.
Montgomery, Sir Hugh, 51.
Moore, Frank, quoted, 65.
More, Major, 17.
Morriftown, 59, 61.
Moylan, Col. Stephen, 11, 15, 17.
Mullan, John, wounded, 16.

NEWARK, N. J., 22.
  New Bridge, 26, 47.

## Index.

ORANGETOWN, 47, 48.

PASSAICK, 26.
Pegasus, 41.
Philips, Thomas, killed, 16.
Piscataway, 57.
Preface, 3.
Preface of London Edition, 1781, 10.
Proctor, Col. Thomas, 10, 15, 17, 20, 26, 31, 48.
Prior's Mills, 6.

RAHWAY River, 56.
Richmond, Staten Island, 62.
Rivington, Card to, 64.
Robison's Ferry, 62.
Rosalinda, Card by, 64.
Rose presented to an Officer, 63, 64.

SARGENT, Winthrop, quoted, 4, 48, 49, 50, 51, 58, 65.
Schralenburgh, 37, 51.
Shannon, 26.
Sharp, Alexander, wounded, 16.
Short Hills, N. J., 52.
Skinner's Corps, 61.
Sloops burnt, 14.
Soupaan, 26, 47.
Spain, Fleets of, 64.
Sparks's Washington quoted, 49.
Springfield, N. J., 52, 58, 63.
Staten Island, 43, 61, 62.
Stewart, Col., 17.
Stirling, Earl of, 32, 61.
Symmes, John Cleves, 63.

TANNER, Gen. Wayne thus called, 25.
Tappan, 26, 47.
Thompson, John, 4.
Tinack, 28, 48, 49.
Tryon, General, 54.

WARD, Capt. Thomas, 3, 15, 17, 22, 23.
Washington, General, 4, 5, 7, 10, 11, 17, 34, 48, 50, 52
Wayne, Gen. Anthony, 3, 6, 10, 11, 12, 15, 17, 18, 20, 25, 27, 29, 31, 32, 39, 40, 41, 45, 47, 65.
White Plains, 51.
Withrington, 35, 50.
Woromb, Col., 63.

YAGERS, 59.

www.ingramcontent.com/pod-product-compliance
Lightning Source LLC
Chambersburg PA
CBHW020252090426
42735CB00010B/1894